Common Sense Life Hacks

A Survival Guide to Achieving Your Goals And Improving Your Business And Personal Relationships

A.L. Harlow

DISCLAIMER AND TERMS OF USE AGREEMENT:

The authors offer no warranties regarding the accuracy or completeness of this book. If you wish to use any ideas contained in this book you are assuming responsibility for your actions.

Neither the authors nor the publisher will be held liable for any direct, indirect, punitive or consequential damages arising from the use of any the material, contained in this book. This book is provided without warranties.

This work is © Copyrighted by Mangon Publications. No part of this work may be copied, or changed in any format, or used in any way other than what is outlined in this book. Any violations would be prosecuted severely.

Table Of Contents

Introduction

Everybody wants to succeed in life. Success is everybody's dream. Unfortunately though, it is not presented on a silver platter. The pursuit of success is the driving factor of most people's lives. Humans simply want better in their lives.

This book contains two hundred tips to help you to better your life and improve personal and business relationships. If you follow these tips you will be empowered and equipped to attain whatever realistic goals you set.

Here's some simple advice that has been given to many people; "If you do as you've always done you will get as you've always gotten."

My personal motto is comprised of ten two letter words: If It Is to Be It Is up To Me.

The Grand Idea

Maintain The Proper Mindset

The right attitude must be maintained whether you are building a business or driving to work. Maintaining a good attitude is and always will be the number one precondition for achieving your goals. And frankly, it is the sole qualification that you will need.

Be Interested And Listen

Knowledge is power and if you are not listening, you will lack knowledge. Without knowledge you quite simply will have no direction. You don't have to know everything but it matters a lot to know what does matter.

Maintain Your Good Health

Do not be silly enough to think that you can make it on by intelligence alone. Consume proper amounts of food and water. If you neglect your health you can never accomplish your goal.

Use Your Common Sense

Here's a truth that smarts to hear or read about. Data has piled up on the amount of people who lose everything they have because they didn't use common sense. It is pre-programmed into everybody and using it actually makes life in general much easier.

Smile a Lot

It's true! Smiling goes above almost all differences. Just think how much it would benefit your cause. It is not the most trivial of signals. Smiling is something that works to your benefit. This has been proven time after time.

Individual Happiness

Show Appreciation Of The Little Things
Look for reasons to be happy. It doesn't have to be a special person or a new car. In truth, you will be amazed at how little things can touch you in big ways.

Take In The Smell Of The Coffee
Seriously, the aroma of coffee brewing can turn up your nerves and make a more beautiful day.

Get Out And Ride A Bicycle
Riding a bicycle is a thrill that never gets old. In fact, it is like wine; it gets better in time. Another thrill is that, not only will it delight your insides; you will look modish pedaling all over town.

Take Your Shoes Off And Walk Barefoot Once In A While
But don't step on broken glass. Walk barefoot at the beach and in and around your home. Yes you will have dirty soles but also a happy experience.

Stretch Far Out While You Yawn
Refraining from yawning during a meeting is important but rising up from slumber and stretching is something else. Extend your arms as to the point you can almost hear your muscles contracting.

Take A Bubble Bath To Relax

Take bubble baths. Enhance the experience by placing scented candles in the bathroom. Scented candles will help to create a calming, serene ambiance helping you to enjoy the sensations.

Scream As Loudly As You Can

To strengthen your positive energies first you must let go of your negative energies. Scream as loudly as you can to release your adverse energies and make room for your constructive energies.

Star Gaze

Not the ones in movies or sports, stars like the big dipper, the Southern Cross and other constellations are far better to gaze at. Get away from the city lights, lay flat on the ground, unwind and revel in the company of millions of stars and imagine they are all twinkling for you.

Sing Along With Your Favorite Track

Humming a tune is okay but singing aloud is more satisfying. You do not have to do it in public; the shower is a good place. Just put on your favorite CD and sing along with the music.

Talk With A Toddler

When they are not annoying, children are the most humorous creatures on planet earth. Not only can they take the simplest things and make a big deal out of them, unlike your spouse, they can do it in a way that is non-irritating and ridiculously funny.

Have Sex

Enjoy mind blowing sex with someone in places where you have never done it before. It doesn't have to be a night long marathon; one great orgasmic experience will really make you happy.

Set Realistic Goals

Put Your Priorities On Paper
Written goals as opposed to thoughts will help you considerably. First create a guideline and read or even modify it daily. Arrange your list of goals in the order you want to achieve them.

Remove Them One At A Time
Don't be in a hurry to erase all your likes and dreams. Fulfill your goals one by one. Remember, the longer it takes the sweeter the success will be.

Set Achievable Goals
If you have $20 million dollars to spare, you can shoot for the stars. If you don't then maybe it is better to dwell on something else. It will be much easier that way. Not because you fear a challenge, it's just that setting achievable goals will bring you closer to success. If you have a goal to increase your income and you presently earn $500.00 per week, don't set a goal of $2000.00 per week. Start with $600.00 per week and raise it when you have achieved that goal.

Keep Your Goals To Yourself
When you set your goals don't tell anybody who does not support you 100%. Telling non-supportive people is counter-productive. Non-supportive people will fill your head with doubts by telling you all the reasons you cannot achieve your goals. Oh, they mean well when

they say be careful or no-one I know has ever done that but they are speaking from ignorance.

Fess Up To Your Mistakes
It is said that when one accepts that they have made a mistake they are superhuman.

Recognize Your Support Group
Never, ever, forget who the people were that helped you get where you are. Show the gratitude as you progress and thank them again when you achieve your goal.

Set Your Time lines
I want to earn more money and I want to be earning more money within six months is two very different goals. One is vague and the other is clearly defined. You must prioritize your goals and know which goals need to be achieved within a certain time frame. Procrastination is your biggest enemy in achieving your goals. People do not generally fail due to one big mistake, they fail due many seemingly minor things they did not do.

Seek Assistance When You Need It
Attempting something a few times is to be expected but failing several times means it is time to ask for help. Recognize when you need assistance because the more time you spend trying and failing, the more disappointed you will feel and the sooner you will give

up. The point at which you gave up was the point at which you failed.

Accept The Inevitability Of Criticism
Nobody relishes criticism of their efforts but criticism is inevitable. Rather than brooding about criticism use the critique to your benefit or even better still, prove to those who criticize you that you are better than they think.

Embrace A Friendly Competition
Charles Darwin in his "Origins Of Life", postulated that people are designed to try to better each other. If he was correct, it makes no sense to try to stop it now. However, this time, make it a friendly competition.

Celebrate Your Successes
Oftentimes we forget to acknowledge ourselves when we succeed in achieving a goal. That is an unbalanced approach that lets you hold the championship without recognition. Reward yourself as you achieve each goal.

Do It For You
Participate in a decathlon because you choose to do it for you, not because somebody else is doing it or somebody else wants you to do it. You will never attain self-satisfaction if you allow other people or trends to dictate what you do.

Money Matters

Identify The Source Of Your Income
The prerequisite to financial security is recognizing your source(s) of income. By recognizing this you will identify not only when you will have money but also how much you will have etc. Setting budget restrictions will restrain the way you spend money.

Open More Than One Bank Account
You must maintain different bank accounts for emergencies, long-term savings and your daily expenses. Setting limits on each will secure your future and restrict unnecessary spending.

Never Spend More Than You Have
Credit cards are wonderful but they only teach people to bite off more than they can chew. Do not use credit cards they only serve to create high interest debt.

Only Saving Will Not Increase Your Money
Start a business, buy stocks or start trading. There are many ways to add value to what you have. It is not just about having money in the bank, the bigger picture is knowing how to put that money to work generating more money.

Employ A Bookkeeper

Anyone who tells you to manage your own finances is giving you the worst "saving" tip. DIY is admirable, but when dealing with money it is safer to trust an expert.

You Must Treat Money Differently

One of the things wealthy people do is use their money to experience different things. Having millions in the bank may have a feel good factor but possessing money and not being able to buy a new car, travel or indulge in the pleasures that money can buy is a poor disadvantage.

Do Not Lend Your Money

There is one good reason to not lend anybody your money. You may or may not get it back. This does not imply that you should be greedy but it is really helpful to be careful when you choose whom to help.

Buy Insurance

Be financially sensible and protected by insuring your goods. It is cheap coverage for valuable assets.

Money Does Not Grow On Trees

Whether the money was inherited or worked for, you must do something to keep the cash earning and flowing. It may be surprising to you to hear how penny-wise the wealthy are when they are on a shopping trip. When you have more money don't be mister big spender. Make better deals with suppliers by learning and practicing the art of bargaining to get a fair and reasonable price.

Be Humble

Money may buy many things but it does not give wealthy people the right to act uncaringly.

Intellect

Listen In On Others Conversations

Listening to the conversations of others is undeniably impolite but pretending you are not invalidating them in your head is more thought-provoking than talking out loud. The great thing about listening to other's conversations is that though you may not know what they are talking about you learn hoping that it is not just gossip.

Read All The Signs

It is surprising how much information you can get by reading the signs. Rather than just walking past, read the signs on cafes, buildings or billboards.

Go To The Library

Visit a library, choose a desk and watch the people focused on their study. Visit a library not only to check the books but also to accept the concept that learning a few things is smart.

Write A Love Letter

Composing messages arouses your mind. In today's world where communication is frequently short, writing an amorous letter will exercise your vocabulary and stimulate you to want to know more inventive expressions to share your emotions.

Finish Reading A Book

Simply reading a page or two is vastly dissimilar to finishing a book. Books frequently leave one speculating and time and again that is sufficient to make you want to know more.

Debate With Someone

Pose questions, express your point or just discuss current matters. Listening to yourself converse and noticing how others recognize you and your ideas is the simplest way to measure your intelligence.

Don't Be Too Shy To Ask

Menus can occasionally be perplexing, so if you find yourself stuck choosing between steak and potato of fish and chips while on a dinner date, don't be afraid to ask.

Listen To Audiobooks

Whilst driving you could be learning a new language; audiobooks are frequently useful in correcting both wording and enunciation. There are many audiobooks on many subjects you can select from so you can listen to what you enjoy.

Scan The Daily Papers

Don't flip through to the sports page, even if you don't like it, take time to peruse the other news and business sections. You may pick a new word or latch onto the particulars of a story everyone has been talking.

Talk To People

Converse with other people, tell them what your interests are and listen to what they have to say. You can find body language, declarations and even facial responses that you may or may not like.

Healthy Living

Drink Lots Of Water
Water is critical for sustaining normal body functions; everybody should drink the recommended eight glasses of water daily.

Start Eating Your Vegetables
Vegetables don't only provide your body with vitamins and minerals they also deliver fiber to ensure good digestion. Eat your vegetables to maintain good health and fend off diseases.

Get Plenty Of Exercise
Today, a growing number of people suffer from illnesses as a direct result of an inactive lifestyle and unless you want to be one of them, start moving.

Give Up Tobacco
It only requires one puff on a cigarette to reduce the ability of your blood vessels to deliver fresh oxygenated blood throughout your body. The more dependent you are on nicotine, the more animated you feel but your insides pay a hefty price.

Eat A Good Breakfast
Never go without breakfast. A bowl of porridge or a couple of slices of toast with eggs will provide you with enough nutrition and control your weight while you're not even looking.

Sleep During The Night

You may think that taking power naps during the day is the equivalent of doing it at night but you will be thinking wrong. You will not only gain more weight but also you increase your chances of having a headache.

Try To Avoid Too Many Drugs

Legal or not, a high content of drugs in your system is a severe problem. High drug content destroys your liver and debilitates your mind, Worst of all they create dependency. The next time you're inclined to pop a Tylenol, why not try resting your body until the pain dissipates?

Maintain Good Hygiene

Bathe regularly, brush your teeth after eating and change your clothes. These are the fundamentals in the fight against diseases.

Take Supplements

Do yourself a favor by taking extra minerals and vitamins. Vitamin E is for strong hair and tighter skin, Vitamin B helps with brain activity and Iodine works to control your thyroid.

Go Natural When You Can

No I am not saying join a nudist colony. Homeopathic treatments have become more popular than before. Treat yourself to a cup of tea or coffee, a relaxing massage and some time to detox. These all revitalize and purify your body of damaging contaminants that are contained within the many processed foods that people eat today.

Social Conduct

Take A Taxi
An all-night drinking binge is okay but driving afterwards is just plain stupid. Not only can it cause an accident, it can totally ruin your future or even take the life of another.

Protect Yourself
Not all women and men are careful about their sexual encounters. Remember, when you have sex with one person, by extension you are having sex with others that person has been with. So, if you do not want to get knocked up, get someone else knocked up or catch a nasty disease always insist on using protection. It is for the benefit of both of you.

Pay Your Taxes
Though nobody really likes it, the essence of being a citizen is paying your taxes. Pay what you owe and pay it on time. Why, because it keeps you out of trouble.

Cultivate Friendships
Friendships are what make life interesting, easier and more enjoyable. Don't abuse someone's friendship and don't allow others to abuse yours. Life delivers many fair weather friends but few real friends.

Respect Authority

You may get away with not showing your parents much respect but out in the real world, unless you enjoy conflict, it is the only suitable way to go. If you want respect you must first give respect. Keep that in mind because it is a system that works.

Basic Survival:
Tips For Life In General

Stay Calm

Nothing in life is guaranteed to go as planned 100% of the time. Often things turn out differently than planned. When faced with a plan not working as intended you must tackle the circumstances with much skill as you can. Take a deep breath, analyze the situation and make a decision. But do it calmly.

Face The Issues

It is pointless to avoid issues; they will not just go away. Whatever the problem and no matter how worrying or difficult it is, confronting it head on is the only way to get it resolved. Whatever you choose to do may or may not be the best approach but at least you did not run and bury your head in the sand.

Be Strong

Simply not surrendering often solves many problems. Summon the power to make it work and solicit the help of professionals or friends if needs be. Giving up is the way of the weak not the winner.

How To Become An Effective Worker

Check Yourself Out

You only get one chance to make a first impression. Presence is the whole enchilada, if you want to get the job then present yourself in a professional and appealing way. Create the look that says you are the person they are looking for.

Know What You Are Getting Into

Never enter an interview without knowledge of the company you want to work for and an understanding of the job you are applying for. How great you look and how highly recommended you are will not help if you come with no knowledge. The interview process is a two sided coin; you must check them out and they just might check you in.

Be Professional

Whether it be white collar or blue when applying for a job you must always look and act professionally. Dress up not down, shave, get a haircut and wear clean tidy clothing.

Follow Through

Employers never forget what applicants say when they interview. So if you want to keep the job you had better impress your employer by doing what you said you would do. Remember, getting the job is the easy part, keeping the job, not so.

Do Your Job

You cannot be considered an employee if you do not perform like an employee. Showing up for work on time is one of those things. Whether you work in a building or on-line "showing up" means the same thing.

Achieve Goals

If it is only about the salary you will be dragging your ass to work much like a prostitute. One path to becoming a valued employee is to set and achieve goals. Doing this will not only ensure you rewarding bonuses, it will satisfy your professional needs as well.

Be A Team Player

Do you want to get a promotion? Well, it will only happen if you show your employer that you are a team player who can work with their coworkers successfully. Moving up in any employment means demonstrating that you know how to move around the team well enough to produce results.

Show Them What You Still Have

When you are seeking a raise or promotion you will be judged on accomplishments not how long you have been on the job. Always be ready to impress your employer with new forward looking ideas that reflect what they know of you.

Be Prepared To Ask For It

Waiting and expecting is not always the best way to go. If you really want that promotion, be prepared to ask for it. This will not only display your confidence to take on the position, it will also show your readiness to face the challenge of proving your worth.

Show Respect

Always be respectful to all people. Whether it is about opinions or tastes it is especially important when employees answer to you.

Learn From Those Who Came Before

The best teacher you will ever find is experience. Experience does not always have to be your own. By using the experience and wisdom of others you will open yourself to ideas that you may never have imagined.

Relationships

Business Relationships:
Partners and Customers Draw The Line

Attachments of the wrong kind frequently destroy the best relationships. Thus, one should always define boundaries at the beginning. Defining boundaries not only keeps things in check but prevents damage control.

Be Legal

Never mix business and pleasure together. For any business relationship to work, both partners must always retain a lawyer and an accountant. Not only will these two people protect the company from failing, they will also hopefully prevent internal disputes. One piece of good advice, most partnerships end in bloodshed, figuratively speaking. If you have a friend now, go into business together and there is a 99% chance your friendship will soon end.

Do Not Be Ignorant

Don't just invest financially in a business. Devote some of your time to study the market and the position of your business or simply be present if you need to be.

Gain The Trust Of Your Customers

Investors are continually guarded regarding their fellow investors so leave the attitude in the boardroom. The only way a business can prosper is by developing a relationship of trust with their clients/customers. You can only build a business by delivering on your promises.

Value And Seek Out Feedback
Ask customers how you're doing. Continue doing what they report as positive and fix whatever the think is negative. Growing businesses crave feedback and successful businesses need reassurance.

Be Open To Compromise
Poorly managed business or personal relationships can effortlessly be ruined by doubts. These would be doubts about work share, profit and other money matters. For any business relationship to work, all or both partners must be willing to accept and practice the art of compromise.

Personal Relationships:
Family, Friendship and Intimate

Be Committed
Commitment is a prerequisite of all kinds of relationships, without it, any relationship will surely fail. Whether it be at work, in school or with one's family, you must obligate yourself to perform your side of the bargain.

Know When To Reciprocate
Countless relationships fail due to partners not knowing how to respond appropriately. There are no set-in-cement rules to developing or fostering a

relationship, you simply need to let go and let your feelings take over.

Realize The Need To Communicate
If you sincerely want your partnership to be a success, then you had better become proficient in the arts of talking and listening. And listen twice as much as you talk.

Be Creative
A dull and boring relationship is as welcome as a wet fart. You must look for ways to stimulate, generate curiosity and inject life to whatever you have. Families need vacations, friends need catching up with.

Be Yourself
Close family, friends, couples and business partners should never be less than honest with each other. Pretense does not work for either side.

Show Some Love
Simply being a part of a family is not sufficient, children habitually long for their parents to hug them or pat them on the back. It is easy to say "I love you" but that is not the same as showing someone you love them. Friends need more than just having fun times. Always treat your lover in the best way you know how.

Mentoring Relationships:
Recognize The Purpose Of The Relationship

Training programs work best if all parties involved recognize the purpose of the relationship. You must produce a methodology that is hospitable, carefully thought out and well executed.

Set A Time Frame

To achieve better outcomes, teacher - student relationships must create a schedule that is both suitable and attainable.

Do Not Judge Others

Nobody likes every person they meet but in such a kind of relationship one must not pass judgment on others.

Have Fun

Relax, let loose and have fun.

Be Generous

Urge and reassure your subordinate by frequently praising his or her performance. The only way a mentoring relationship will ever work is if you freely give honest observations and proposals in order to more effectively achieve goals.

How To Win With Everyday Agonies

Be Patient

If the line at the coffee counter is long, don't fret simply wait for your turn. If the bus is overdue cool your heels and sit tight it will come eventually. Inconveniences are things that happen daily, instead of resenting every minute of them, just extend your patience and things will eventually fall in place. Getting upset and stressed over it will not change anything external.

Lousy Boss

At one or more points in one's life, he or she will be convinced that they have boss from hell. Welcome to the club but get beyond your angst or quit your job because they will be coming to work every day. Why spend time and mental anguish thinking and talking about how you would be a better boss when it is not going to get you anywhere?

No More Hot Water

You have overslept and find there is no hot water in the shower and God forbid, none for your coffee either. Throwing a tantrum, stomping your feet may help you express your feelings but what is the point?

Empty Promises

Few things in life disturb me more that empty promises. Some people just never get the concept of promptness. You hear nothing but "I'm sorry" or "I'll do better tomorrow." This is really exasperating so instead of listening to the same BS every day, just be straight, tell them it is the last time and fire the person if you have to.

Horrible Date

You wanted to enjoy a perfect date night but you ended up with a horrible evening. This, sadly, is one of the pitfalls of dating and as bad as it may appear, other than being rude and walking away, which I do not recommend, there is nothing you can do, so laugh it out and eat and drink the night away.

Age Is Just A Number

Stop counting the years because no one else is asking. Besides that, the more you worry about it, the more you will look like it.

Shift Your Focus

Use your common sense and participate in activities that will keep you fit.

Never Stop Learning

Though how you look may be the first thing that people observe it may not always be the asset that endures. There is no ceiling on what you can learn as long as you never stop.

Travel To Far Off Places

Travel as much as you can until you can no longer do it. Gain the experience of different cultures, visit destinations you've never been to. Don't go to the same place every weekend or on every vacation, expand your reach.

Give Back

The prizes of giving back to your community are more beneficial than one would ever imagine. You don't have to be Bill Gates and build a foundation or anything that grandiose, but choosing a cause to work for and keeping it up will categorically bust those aging blues and boost your self-esteem.

Laugh Out Loud

People often forget to laugh. The more immersed with life people get, the less chances they have to hang out, do exciting things and even laugh. The benefits of laughing are innumerable so for someone who can't find a single reason to laugh is laughable itself.

What To Do When Things Did Not Go As Expected

Allow Yourself To Grieve

Any time one loses a loved one is very difficult but withholding tears is even worse. Release your pain; cry, wail or scream. The process of grieving is natural so do not be stoic and try to keep it bottled up.

Talk To Someone About It

It may not be easy but sharing how you feel with someone else is more important than you might think. Cultivating the pain, hurt and angst can oftentimes be more than one can deal with alone. So before you collapse, seek the help of a sympathetic person who will take the time to listen to you.

Visit Their Grave

Visiting the grave of recently dead love ones will help with acceptance, release and closure. Often it helps us to realize that they have transcended to a better place.

Pray, Have Quiet Time Or Meditate

Meditation or prayer is something many find comforting. Just find a quiet place where you will have solitude and do your thing. This is often the only way to comfort your grieving self.

Forgiveness Is For You

When someone is responsible for the demise of your loved one it is often challenging to move beyond it. Forgiving is not only noble but also the best way to move on. The person you are blaming is not the one suffering, you are. So the act of forgiveness is for your own benefit.

It Is Not A Unique Situation

People often suffer from broken hearts so what makes you think your case should be any different? Though it is always difficult, relationships do end although it may not have ended the way you would prefer, it is what you got. But hey, it has happened to others too.

Get A Closure

Without closure you can never really move beyond a relationship. Without closure you are kept insecure and most importantly, waiting longer.

Fix It

Not all damaged relationships are meant to finish. If you are certain that you are simply going through a rough patch then try to fix it. Don't just give up.

Meet Up With New People

Getting to know new people or socializing with friends is the fastest way to move beyond a dysfunctional relationship. This is not being heartless, but there is no sense in waiting around.

Lower Your Pride

Love is often accompanied by pride and oftentimes, it is the selfish sense of self that ruins a good relationship. When the water gets rough as it sometimes will, make sure you are aware of when to wave a white flag. Be the first to apologize, it is a sign of strength not weakness.

Look For A New Job

Today it does no good to mope. With deteriorating economies and intensified use of new technologies, people are getting the short straw. Instead of complaining about it, whip up a new C.V. and focus on getting another job.

Develop A New Skill.

Reinvent yourself by learning a new skill set. With rising unemployment and fewer jobs you must stay ahead of the pack by adding value to yourself.

This Is Not A Time To Be Choosy

Maybe you are super talented but if you are not then you cannot risk being picky. Even an MBA degree cannot promise a white collar job in today's market. So if you ever find yourself with choices below your expectations, it may be best to take the job and make the best out of it whilst you seek something else.

Have More Than One Job

Since times are hard and money is tight, what's wrong with working two jobs? You could have one that is fun and another that pays better. This way you will be kept amused and financially buoyant.

Adjust Your Lifestyle

When you find yourself struggling to get back on your feet it may be time to re-think your lifestyle. Failing to alter your standard of living will limit your choices of new employment and incur more debt.

When The Problem Is You

Accept The Blame

Many people have difficulty accepting the blame for things they have done. However, denying or refuting the allegations only creates a bigger mess. Alleviate your circumstances by acknowledging the charges and cooperating with authorities to bring a quick resolution to the issue.

Don't Create Stories

Often people who are at fault tend to fabricate lies. Though fabrication of the truth is a common reaction it only delays solving the problem.

Offer The Truth

Situations are never fixed with simply catching perpetrators in the act. If you find yourself involved in a situation, truthfully explain yourself. Although this will not absolve you of your wrongdoing, it will shine a better light on why this happened.

Subject To Correction

The rehabilitation process does not occur overnight or within days. Contingent on the seriousness, you may even have to spend time in prison, a treatment facility or confined to your house. Punishment is often the only effective way of getting people to fully realize the crime or offense they committed.

Do Not Lose Hope

Wishing and praying for a better conclusion is not against the law. Desiring an exit from the situation is also not bad because it will all happen in time. Hope is a good thing to hold onto. In fact, hope may be what keeps you alive.

Do Not Live In The Past

After serving your sentence, completing a treatment regimen or recovering from your wounds, walk away with your head held high. Though it may not be a happy memory but don't let yesterday control tomorrow. Make your peace, get over it and start afresh.

Steer Away From Trouble

Whatever it takes, don't let yourself follow the same path. If you do find yourself back in the same place, simply turn your back and walk away.

Dealing With Loneliness

Think About Something Else
The worst recipe is loneliness and being alone. If you are strong enough try not to dwell on the situation by thinking about something else. If you find that nobody is responding to your pleas for help, talk to the mirror but don't do it to the point of being psychotic.

Answer The Question
Oftentimes, people find themselves alone because of things they did themselves yet they fail to recognize this because they prefer to concentrate on their bruised feelings and self-pity. Ask yourself this question, "why did this happen to me?" If you are truthful with yourself the answer can often put an end to your misery.

Find A New Love
Make yourself feel better by getting involved with another person. This may or may not deliver a satisfactory outcome, but at least you tried.

Call A Friend
Pick up the telephone and call a friend. Bodily separation can easily be repaired with a simple phone call.

Watch Some Television
If your loneliness does not have you at the point of breaking down and detesting yourself turn on the

television and forget that you are alone wherever that may be.

Think Of It As A Break

Private time with oneself is often hard to come by. This is especially true if you are the kind who enjoys working and socializing. The mere thought of being alone might be scary. Why not just think of it as a break and private time.

Decide To Make It Your Choice

From time to time, some people are really destined to be alone. Being alone may not be as bad as people consider it to be. If you happen to be alone for a lengthy period assess the circumstance, maybe it is the way you want your life to be.

End It

To flounder in loneliness is not easy but at some time you will outgrow the circumstances. It might take a while, maybe weeks, months or even years to happen but when it does, end your struggle and carry on.

Suicidal Tendencies

Do Not Take Suicidal Thoughts Lightly.
Having thoughts of suicide is never a normal thing. If you discover yourself considering suicide, cry loudly for help immediately.

Google The Signs.
If you can still control your thoughts, do some research on the Internet or ask someone about it. Also, you could check out one of our other books about depression here:

www.mangonpublications.com

Stay Away From Drugs And Booze.
This should be a "no-brainer". Depressive thoughts will get worse when mixed with too much drinking, partying and drugs. It is vitally important to be active and healthy if you are having these feelings.

Never Spend Time Alone.
It is not easy to confide to a close friend that you are suffering with suicidal thoughts so prevent yourself from being alone. Pitiful as it may seem, always seek reasons to stay with another person until you are ready to talk about it.

Tell Yourself That It Is A Crazy Thought.

As frequently as you can, argue with yourself and keep telling yourself: this is crazy thinking, this is crazy thinking.

Show Recognizable Signs.

If you cannot vocalize your thoughts, display some outward indications that you are struggling within. Do something odd and unlike you to get other people taking a second look at you.

Submit Yourself To Treatment.

Visit your doctor and talk about your suicidal thoughts. Suicidal tendencies cannot be dealt with by yourself, so keep yourself alive by getting help immediately.

Help Others By Talking About It.

Think of yourself as fortunate when you have succeeded in controlling your suicidal thoughts. Afterwards, if you are willing, talk to your friends and family about how you beat it.

Be Cautious.

A person suffering with suicidal thoughts must never leave their support group. You can never know when the thoughts might return.

Inhibited By Inhibitions: Break Free

Who Is It?

Finding the causes of your inhibitions is way to solve them. Are you shy around girls? Find the reason. Maybe it is because you want to impress but you don't know how.

Find A Reason To Get Closer.

If you find you cannot get near someone, look for an excuse to get close short of forcing yourself to. For instance, you could attend the same class or get a friend to set up something. Just invent a plausible way to suddenly find yourself near the person.

What Is Holding You Back?

If you are not comfortable with the idea of approaching someone or bringing up your topic during a meeting, ask yourself "what is it that makes the thought suffocate me?" If it is fear of being ignored or proven wrong, then make an effort to double check your topic to save yourself from embarrassment.

Are You An Over Thinker?

If you are the kind of person who thinks too much you are more than likely having a difficult time approaching anyone else. Over rationalization is no good because you have probably played the scene out in your head over and over so many times that you find no reason to make your point out loud.

Just Do It.

Simply go and do it. Continually thinking about doing it but falling apart just by thinking about it is so frustrating that it can stop you in your tracks. After all the procrastination and going in circles, just do it and don't look or turn back until you have reached your goal.

Don't Let Your Ego
Get The Best Of You

Watch Me, I Am So Good.
If you want to be acknowledged for something, don't desire it too much.

You Were Not Too Bad Yourself.
If you are only saying "you were not too bad yourself" to get your associate to emphasize on what you did, then you are simply attempting to feed your ego in a bad way. Pretty soon, your friends will start to take notice of how you play the conversation and will stop playing with you.

I Am Better Than You Because.
If you are acting like you are superior to your friends because you got a promotion or an award for something is a big taboo.

Me, Me and Me.
If you are the type who always wants to talk about yourself and even though no one has asked, or if you must always insert a sentence or two about how you did it that is super annoying. If you find that you are the only one speaking at the table, it may be because you just took over with on one of your famous monologues.

Top Ten Virtues You Must Adapt

Commitment: An Enthusiastic Zeal.
Commitment in any relationship prevents you being an infidel. It maintains your allegiance to your employer or partner and of course, your enthusiasm to simply improve your life.

Grace: Keeping It All In.
Despite all the toil and trouble in life, you must adapt to a life of grace. Beauty is unnecessary if you project grace because with grace everything else glows easily.

Love, Love, Love.
Love is the most wholesome emotion of all. Love is exactly what you require to make you desire better things.

Mercy: Knowing When To Be Powerful.
Comprehending the notion of forgiveness is one thing acting on it and showing mercy is another. This is a cruel world we live in and in it, mercy is the saving grace. Forgiving another persons transgressions is for your benefit not theirs.

Sensitivity: A Touching Asset.
Knowing the right moment to react and how to act a certain situation is paramount; especially between

persons who feel they have insufficient influence to express their needs out loud.

Wonder: Insatiable Curiosity.
Despite failing situations, nothing revitalizes the human spirit than constant amazement.

Service: Giving Back When It Matters.
The ability and willingness to help others is very potent medicine for satisfying your inner self. Service to others is an act that will always bring a smile to every one's faces.

Knowledge: The Power To Reason.
Knowledge of what to do, how to react, when to answer and how to do them is an important thing to possess in times of pleasure and discomfort. The ability to process an idea is the only thing that has separates humans from other creatures. Continuously hone your intelligence by nourishing your mind with thoughts, ideas and information.

Joyfulness: A Smile To Give
Life is not always easy, so finding a motivation to smile is as important as physique and intellect.

Regaining Your Strength

Find New Meaning.
Though this may sound implausible, particularly when you have reached the bottom rung, it is probably what you most need to hear or read. It does not imply that you must find new love immediately; it simply means get out there and have fun.

Redefine Your Goals.
If you find yourself starting all over again it is best to change everything. Start from what you want to achieve in life. Failure can be difficult to deal with but constantly thinking about it is the worst. It is good to keep in mind that you have not failed until you quit. Up to the point of quitting, every perceived failure is actually and education; you learned what does not work.

Let The Past Stay In The Past.
Dwelling on the past will get you nowhere and oftentimes, you can never really progress without letting all your feelings go. The past is done and finished so encumbering yourself with it is a waste of valuable time that will rob you of viable years.

Rehabilitate Your Mind And Body.
Get some therapy if you need to but work on your muscles and brain activity to restart things.

It Is For Your Ego.

Your ego is the nurturer of your self-worth. Getting a makeover is a perfect way to restock it.

It Changes Your Aura.

Have you noticed that just getting a haircut makes other people look twice and say, "There is something new with you and it is not just the hair".

It Is Self--Satisfying.

Getting a makeover is a very selfish act of gratification and you simply must have one to enjoy your life and live healthier.

Take Up A New Hobby.

Try stepping out of your comfort zone. Learn a new sport, team up with new people and sweat it out like a professional.

Get A New Wardrobe.

Having the courage to wear an outfit that you have previously avoided may be challenging at first but with the advice of a fashion guru, you just might be able to pull it off. When you see the enchantment in another person's eye it will assuredly increase your confidence and compel you to dare more.

Delete Your Facebook Page.

Continually being reminded of your troubled past will extend your healing time. I know social network sites can be fun but some people just do more harm than good with their heartless comments. If they are non-supportive deactivate or delete them today to avoid further pain.

Get A Pet

Go to the animal shelter and select a dog or cat that you like. It has been proven time and again that an animals' presence is a potent advantage to help overcome grief, depression or even simple misfortunes.

Hit Something, (Like a Pillow)

Let your pent up emotions out by making a fist and punching something. Yes, I know, a person's face would be more satisfying but that can send land you in jail.

Stroke The Brush

You don't need to rival Picasso when you do some painting, just do it to see how you respond to the play of colors. Colors often prompt people to recall happier thoughts. Sometimes this is enough to revive a lost soul.

Go To India

India has more people crowded together than any place on earth. Upon arrival it is possible to lose yourself. Sometimes, you just need to go somewhere where there is so much life that it causes you to recognize how infinitesimal and doleful your concerns are. India is also a spiritual place where it is possible to revitalize both your mind and body.

Learn To Say No

Sometimes people are overly polite, so polite that they can't resist saying yes rather than NO. People are commonly being taken advantage of because they can't just say NO. Don't keep satisfying everybody else by denying yourself. Here is a book I read years ago to solve this issue:

https://www.amazon.com/When-I Say-No-I Feel-Guilty-ebook/dp/B004IK8Q22/

Do Something Radical

Go and get a tattoo, color your hair or go to Vegas. Look at it like your last hurrah before rebuilding yourself anew.

End Of The Road:
Zoning In On What You Have

Take Control of Your Life.
Forget about the "yes buts" and "what ifs" just take over your principles and make them real. If it's a new job you want, then go and find one rather than postponing and daydreaming about how well you will perform in your interviews and evaluations.

Discipline Yourself.
If you don't like being fat, eat healthier foods. If you want your employer to pay you more, work on impressing the boss by increasing your value and if you want to start anew then get off your ass and start taking action.

Tame Your Temper.
Control your annoyance about something or someone. Focus your attention on other things rather than dwelling on your growing aggravation. An even better idea is to just know when to walk away.

Be Concerned.
Become aware of the reality that you must care to find your calling. No matter how much or often you proclaim that you can survive without help, or that you don't care; you just may end up fooling only yourself.

Take Some Time Off.

One of the primary causes of people failing in a big way is that they do not know when and how to take a break. If you find yourself on your second, third or even fourth shot at life, then take some time off to catch your breath and relax so you can get a clear picture of where you are going.

Be Responsible.

Stop blaming everything on the economy, managers and associates.

Accept Your Self

You will never succeed in life if you keep beating yourself down. You must accept who and what you are and work on producing a better you.

You Are Already Enough.

You just have to accept the fact that even though you are not perfect but you are satisfied.

A Preview Of:

DEPRESSION

A SELF-HELP BOOK THAT DEALS WITH DEPRESSION, BIPOLAR AND ANXIETY DISORDERS, TREATMENTS, MEDICATIONS AND NATURAL REMEDIES.

A.L.HARLOW

You Are Not Alone

Depression affects people from all walks of life. Look at this list of famous people who suffered with depression yet still did great things with their lives.

Winston Churchill, Prime Minister of Great Britain. Churchill's term for it, "black dog,".

Patty Duke - Bipolar.

Linda Hamilton –Bipolar

Abraham Lincoln - suffered severe bouts of depression.

Isaac Newton - had several "nervous breakdowns" and great fits of rage.

Jimmy Piersall – Bipolar

Brooke Shields - postpartum depression

Vincent Van Gogh - unstable moods accompanied by manic episodes. He committed suicide aged 37.

Ludwig Von Beethoven – Bipolar disorder.

Jane Pauley – Bipolar.

Historical Understandings Of Depression

There has never been a time in history when depression was not a health problem for people.

Many documents have been written by healers, writers and philosophers throughout history that point to existence of depression.

Melancholia was the initial term used to describe depression and the earliest reports come from ancient Mesopotamian texts. Back then, melancholia was blamed on demonic possession. Thus, the first interpretation of depression was that it was a spiritual illness not a physical one.

Among the ancient Greeks and Romans thinking was divided as to the causes of melancholia. At that time, literature was packed with writings about melancholia being caused by spirits or demons. Other early civilizations including Babylon, China and Egypt also considered melancholia to be a form of demonic possession. The treatment prescribed was beatings, restraint, and starvation with the intent of driving the demons out of the body of the possessed person. Differing in opinion were the early Roman and Greek doctors who believed it was both biological and psychological. The Roman and Greek doctors prescribed massage, music, baths and special diets along with a concoction made from the extract of poppies and donkey's to alleviate the melancholic symptoms.

A Greek physician named Hippocrates, thought that mental illness and personality traits were caused by an imbalance of bodily fluids which he called humors. Four of these humors were documented; black bile, phlegm, yellow bile and blood. Hippocrates further classified mental illness into categories. These categories included melancholia, mania and brain fever. Hippocrates believed melancholia was the result of too much black bile in the spleen and he used bloodletting, exercising, bathing, and dieting to treat the symptoms. In contrast the famous Roman philosopher Cicero professed that melancholia was the result of fear, rage and grief. Cicero's was a mental rather than physical explanation.

Hippocrates influence faded In the final years before Christ and the prevailing belief among cultured Romans was that depression and other forms of mental illnesses were caused by the anger of gods and demons. Cornelius Celsus for instance, believed that shackles, beating and starvation were appropriate treatments. The Persian physician Rhazes, who was the head doctor at Baghdad hospital, in contrast to the Roman view, saw the brain as the center of both mental illness and depression. His treatments involved behavior therapy, rewards for good behavior and hydrotherapy.

During the 14ᵗʰ century when the renaissance began in Italy considerations of mental illness was regarded as both progressive and regressive. Witch-hunts and executions of mentally ill persons were common and conversely some doctors reverted to the Hippocratic views, positively stating that the causes of mental illnesses were natural and that the witches themselves were mentally ill people in need medical treatment.

Anatomy of Melancholy was published by Robert Burton In 1621. In this work, Burton described both psychological and social causes such as fear, poverty and solitude as sources of depression. In his work, the treatment recommended was exercise, diet, travel, distraction, blood-letting, purgatives to remove toxins in the body, bloodletting, music, herbal remedies and marriage.

At the onset of the Age of Enlightenment, depression was thought to be an inherited and resolute weakness of disposition, this in turn led to the belief that people affected with depression should be spurned or locked away. The result of this belief was that most people suffering from a mental illnesses became poor and homeless with some being sent to institutions.

Thankfully we have made a lot of progress in treating depression.

Signs And Symptoms

As in the past, depression, is considered to be more a not so much a variety of moods and conditions rather than a particular illness. None of us will ever go through life without feeling sad at some time by the death of a loved one, the break-up of a relationship, or some other disappointment. Depression due to events such as these is perfectly normal, and unless it is long-standing would not require medical intervention.

Nowadays we see long-term depression, in all its forms, as being a condition of the brain and as such, being treatable, through the correction of chemical imbalances in the brain.

While we see depression as a mental ailment, that is not 100% true. It has been said that the reverse of depression is not so much happiness as it is liveliness. Acute depression often causes lethargy and world-weariness, some people even end up being bed-ridden.

THE NATIONAL INSTITUTE OF MENTAL HEALTH
LISTS THE FOLLOWING SYMPTOMS OF DEPRESSION

Difficulty concentrating
Difficulty remembering details
Difficulty making decisions
Feeling fatigued and lacking energy
Feeling guilty, worthless and helpless
Feeling hopeless or pessimistic
Insomnia
Early-morning wakefulness
Excessive sleeping
Irritability
Restlessness
Lost interest in activities
Lost interest in hobbies
Lost interest in sex
Overeating
Loss of appetite
Persistent sadness
Persistent anxiety
Persistent feelings of emptiness
Thoughts of suicide
Attempted suicide

For more books please visit:

www.Al-Harlow.com